Original title:
The Comedy of the Clearing

Copyright © 2025 Creative Arts Management OÜ
All rights reserved.

Author: Isaac Ravenscroft
ISBN HARDBACK: 978-1-80567-207-4
ISBN PAPERBACK: 978-1-80567-506-8

A Dance with Dappled Sun

Under the trees, shadows prance,
Sunlight flickers, a merry chance.
Squirrels gather, wearing their best,
Nature throws an untamed fest.

Breezes whisper, a giggly tune,
Flowers nodding, a jolly swoon.
Bumblebees buzz, a cheerful throng,
In this bright realm, we all belong.

Grins and Groves

In the grove where laughter grows,
Silly faces, looked like clowns' toes.
Birds chirp jokes, a hoot and a call,
All around, we're having a ball.

The trees join in with rustling glee,
Rusty old benches, oh, the spree!
Swinging with giggles, heartstrings play,
In this realm, we chuckle away.

Chuckles in the Chatters

The brook giggles, splashes in cheer,
Fish poke heads, curious near.
Every ripple, a ticklish grin,
As frogs croak tales, where to begin?

The owls wink with a silent laugh,
Underneath stars' playful craft.
Moonlight dances, a shimmering glow,
Where whispers blend, and chuckles flow.

The Playful Path

On this path where pranks reside,
We trip over roots, in laughter we glide.
Brambles tease, tugging at clothes,
Each step we take, silliness grows.

A rabbit darts, with a cheeky flair,
While daisies wink, without a care.
Footsteps echo, giggles in air,
In this wild wood, joy is laid bare.

A Symphony of Sunbeams

In the meadow, a rabbit prances,
With antics that induce wild glances.
He hops and he skips, a clumsy dance,
While butterflies giggle at his chance.

A squirrel steals nuts, it's quite absurd,
With every leap, its tail gets blurred.
It rounds a tree, then takes a spill,
Chasing a shadow, ah, what a thrill!

A chorus of frogs joins in the fun,
Their croaks like laughter under the sun.
Each note they hit is a muddled cheer,
In this bright space, all woes disappear.

With every sound, the forest sings,
Nature's stage where laughter springs.
A symphony pure, in light we bask,
In this playful world, we can only ask!

Brightness in the Underbrush

In the brush, a fox wears a grin,
Chasing its tail, what a silly spin!
It tumbles and rolls, a furry ball,
The woodland chuckles, oh what a call!

A raccoon with paws, quite full of glee,
Sifting through leaves, what will it see?
It finds a hat, a bumblebee too,
Wearing them both, it bids adieu!

A log rolls over, a snake's surprise,
Its dance is a twist, not one to despise.
With a flick and a zoom, it scampers away,
Leaving the crowd laughing at its play.

In this bright realm, mischief thrives,
Creatures frolic, oh how it drives!
Every chuckle, a moment to share,
In the underbrush where joys declare!

A Playful Breath of Air

In the meadow, giggles float,
A breeze just tickles a passing goat.
Trees whisper jokes, leaves respond,
As laughter gathers, it grows, and it's fond.

Clouds jostle high, like silly hats,
While clowns of nature play with the brats.
Sunlight beams with a cheerful grin,
As shadows dance, let the fun begin!

Jestful Journeys through the Thicket

Through tangled vines, the path is sly,
A squirrel steers cartwheels as birds fly by.
Bushes gossip in whispers quick,
While a rabbit dons a cape, quite slick.

Frogs croak songs, but miss the tone,
The hedgehog hums, all on its own.
Each twist reveals a giggling surprise,
As mischief dances in the sunny skies.

Chortles of the Clearing

In the clearing, chuckles bloom,
Sunflowers grin, dispelling gloom.
A spider spins an oddly shaped web,
Caught in a laugh, it loses its ebb.

Bees buzz in tune, a carefree choir,
While ants form lines to a dance of fire.
The air is thick with silly schemes,
In this world, nothing's as it seems.

Playtime with the Pastoral Whispers

In fields where whispers dance and play,
A sheep breaks into a ballet display.
With each skip and hop, joy's revealed,
As nature spins her vast, fun-filled shield.

The brook giggles, splashing along,
While daisies join in a jovial song.
Every rustle and hum works in pairs,
Where laughter leads, all the spirit flares.

Whimsy Woven with Vines

In a garden where giggles bloom,
Grapes wear glasses, mushrooms loom.
Squirrels juggle acorns with glee,
While daisies dance, wild and free.

Laughter leaps from tree to tree,
As shadows twist in jubilee.
Wind whispers jokes to the leaves,
Nature chuckles as it weaves.

Frolic at Daybreak

At dawn, the sun dons a cheeky grin,
Awakening frogs in a merry din.
They leap from lily pads, hop and play,
Startling snails on their slow ballet.

Chirping birds trade silly tales,
As tiny ants hitch ride on snails.
With each ray, the mischief grows,
A dawn of antics, oh how it flows!

Amusement Amidst the Autumn

Leaves tumble down in vibrant hues,
As squirrels wear their best shoes.
Pumpkins grin from their patchy beds,
With funny hats atop their heads.

Children chase the wind's sly tease,
Collecting laughter like fallen leaves.
The harvest moon gives a wink,
As shadows play in a jolly blink.

Riddles in the Rustle

In the thicket, whispers align,
Birds plot pranks under the pine.
A raccoon dons a mask of fame,
As critters giggle at his game.

Branches shake with a playful dance,
While rabbits prance in a merry trance.
The wind tells tales of the night's spree,
As laughter echoes, wild and free.

Jests on the Jungle's Edge

Under a tree, a monkey swings,
Sipping tea while a parrot sings.
The vines giggle in a leafy twist,
As frogs join in, they can't resist.

Squirrels dart with acorn hats,
Bouncing 'round like silly cats.
Each shadow whispers a clever joke,
While chameleons dance, their colors poke.

A sloth cracks a grin from a branch up high,
As ants form a line, oh so spry.
Laughter echoes from root to vine,
In this wild place, all is divine.

With every joke, the jungle glows,
As laughter radiates from all it knows.
Life's a jest, in this vibrant scene,
Where every creature plays the queen and king.

The Forest's Gentle Mischief

In the heart of green, where the shadows dwell,
Whispers of laughter rise and swell.
A hedgehog juggles berries bright,
While fireflies dance, a glowing light.

The breeze tickles leaves, a playful tease,
As mushrooms giggle beneath the trees.
Frogs wear crowns made of dewy grass,
To rule the pond, a silly class.

Here, the owls hoot in playful tones,
Crafting tales of frogs and their ribbiting moans.
Every twig snaps with a secret sound,
Creating joy that knows no bound.

The forest hums with mischievous glee,
As critters play hide and seek by a tree.
Nature's humor, sweet and rare,
In this realm of fun, none can compare.

Delights Amongst the Ferns

Ferns sway gently, a dance in the breeze,
While ladybugs waltz with graceful ease.
Bumblebees buzz with a comic air,
Creating ripples of joy everywhere.

A rabbit jigs in a patch of clover,
As butterflies flutter, never over.
The nightingale croons a silly song,
In the heart of the woods, where we all belong.

Mice wear hats made of twigs and twine,
With giggles that flow like sweetened wine.
The creek chuckles as it runs along,
Mixing with echoes of nature's throng.

Amongst the ferns, laughter does bloom,
Filling the air with a joyous perfume.
Here every moment invites a grin,
In this realm of fun, where we all win.

Chortles in the Canopy

High above where the branches sway,
Birds chirp jokes throughout the day.
A squirrel shares a tale of woe,
Claiming his stash was stolen, oh no!

Each leaf rustles with a cheeky tease,
As vines giggle with the softest breeze.
Monkeys play tag in a game of chase,
With charming antics that set the pace.

Treetops echo with a joyful cheer,
As laughter summons every creature near.
The owls spin tales with every hoot,
Tickling fancies with every little root.

In the canopy where chortles rise,
Nature's humor fills the skies.
With each bright day and night anew,
The jungle's heart is playful too.

Cheerful Encounters by the Brook

A frog in a top hat, quite out of place,
He jumps with a giggle, full of grace.
Squirrels dance in circles, tails in a whirl,
While the fish in the water do a splashing twirl.

A rabbit with glasses reads tales of old,
The sun spills its laughter, warm and bold.
A butterfly winks, then flitters away,
As daisies chuckle, welcoming the day.

Bees buzz in harmony, cheeky and bright,
Chasing their shadows, what a funny sight!
A duck quacks a riddle, all in good fun,
And nature's chorus keeps singing on the run.

Laughter ripples softly on the brook's clear tide,
With every splash echoing joy, wide and wide.
Together in madness, oh what a scene,
Nature's own comedy, jovial and green.

The Laughing Light

Sunbeams are tickling the leaves on the trees,
As shadows play tag with the light summer breeze.
A gopher in goggles observes from his hole,
While the wind blows a tune, lively and whole.

The daisies are dancers, they sway and they spin,
With each twirl they toss out a giggle and grin.
A ladybug struts in her polka-dot dress,
Creating a fashion show, nothing but finesse.

An owl from a branch gives a chuckle, a hoot,
As rabbits in sneakers perform a cute salute.
Squirrels hold courts, debating the nuts,
With laughter erupting from all of their guts.

With the sunset's glow, all the creatures unite,
They share their best stories until it's twilight.
In this silly gathering, warmth fills the air,
Laughter resounds in the soft evening stare.

Sprightly Stories from Nature's Heart

A brook babbles secrets, oh what do they tell?
Of mischievous pixies that cause quite a swell.
A porcupine giggles at all of the fuss,
While ants form a line, trying hard not to rush.

Happy-go-lucky, the rabbits convene,
To joke about carrots, the silliest scene.
A pale bunny proves to be quite the clown,
Dancing on daisies, he never wears frown.

The moon winks above, as if in on the jest,
While fireflies twinkle, they shine at their best.
A bear, in a top coat, waltzes by night,
While crickets compose tunes that bring sheer delight.

In this woodland theater, nature unfolds,
A tapestry woven with laughter and gold.
Everyone joins in, not a soul's left apart,
For joy is the story that lives in our heart.

Joyful Secrets of the Woodland

Underneath the oaks, where squirrels roam free,
A chipmunk recites poems just for me.
The flowers burst giggles with every petal,
As the world celebrates, life turns to a medal.

A hedgehog, quite shy, rolls up in surprise,
When the woodpeckers knock, he peeks with wide eyes.
The frogs hold a concert, croaking with glee,
Each note makes a ripple in the old willow tree.

The sunbeams split laughter, shining so bright,
Casting shadows of joy that dance in the light.
A painterly scene, where the colors collide,
All share a chuckle, no reason to hide.

The forest's alive with its curious ways,
Magic abounds through the light of the days.
In this woodland retreat, where nature's a muse,
The secrets it whispers, bring joy we can't lose.

Echoes of Joyful Shadows

In the glen where laughter sings,
Shadows dance on silly wings.
A squirrel wearing a tiny hat,
Chases tales where giggles chat.

Beneath the trees, the breeze does tease,
Rustling leaves like playful bees.
A deer prances, quite askew,
Wearing flowers that gleam like dew.

All around, the rabbits play,
Joking 'bout the goofy way.
A frog leapt high, then slipped with grace,
Landed right in a turtle's space.

Echoes ring, the sun is bright,
In this realm of sheer delight.
The shadows chuckle, nature's jest,
In this place we find our rest.

Serenade of Sunlit Leaves

Leaves whisper sweet, a merry tune,
Bouncing light with every noon.
A bird sings with a comical flair,
Making grumpy old trees stare.

Sunbeams sparkle, shadows grow,
Twirling grass with a gentle flow.
A nearby brook giggles and glints,
Playing tricks with glimmering hints.

Blossoms burst in colors bold,
While bunnies knit stories told.
They swap tales of flops and slips,
As butterflies do silly flips.

In the air, there's mischief near,
Carried softly, laughter clear.
Nature's stage, a scene so bright,
A serenade of pure delight.

Revelry in the Glade

In the glade, where joy abounds,
Playful spirits break the bounds.
A hedgehog rolls with such a flair,
Chasing shadows, without a care.

The sun dips low, the sky's aglow,
While crickets join the lively show.
A rabbit hops with a bounding beat,
Twisting through fields on tiny feet.

They celebrate with turns and flips,
Dancing close with joyful quips.
A merry moon begins to rise,
Painting laughter in the skies.

In the revel of the night so deep,
Dreams of fun will softly creep.
Amidst the mirth and wild cheer,
The glade keeps secrets ever dear.

The Jester Amongst the Trees

Underneath the leafy crowns,
A jester skips through greens and browns.
His hat is bright, his smile grand,
Juggling mushrooms with a hand.

The trees all chuckle, swaying low,
As he tells tales, from toe to toe.
A wise old owl rolls eyes with flair,
While squirrels laugh and dance in air.

With every tumble, giggles bloom,
The forest hums with warm perfume.
A waltz of whimsy fills the space,
As nature winks with playful grace.

In this realm of jest and cheer,
Every heart finds joy quite clear.
So come, dear friends, take a chance,
Join the jester in this dance.

A Banter of Blossoms

In the garden where flowers debate,
Petals argue, it's never too late.
Roses claim they're the fairest of all,
While daisies giggle and mock their tall.

Bees buzz in, with opinions so loud,
"Listen here, blooms, you're all quite proud!"
Pansies chime in with a colorful wink,
"Stop the arguing—let's all just think!"

The tulips sway, with their heads held high,
"Let's have a laugh, and live till we die!"
Sunshine tickles each leaf and each stem,
The garden's a stage—come join the mayhem!

Later at dusk, they bloom and they sway,
Under the stars, they dance and they play.
In this theatre of petals, so bright,
Every blossom finds joy in the night.

Quips at Dusk

As the sun bows out, with a wink and a grin,
Crickets start chirping—let the fun begin!
Fireflies flicker, a living delight,
Holding tiny lanterns to banter through night.

"Have you heard the one about the old oak tree?"
"I can't keep still, I spill my own tea!"
Laughter erupts from the shadows so deep,
With chuckles of creatures just waking from sleep.

The moon rolls in, a bold, silver face,
Joining the jesters of twilight's embrace.
"Why don't we dance?" says the sly little bat,
"Come join in the fun—no need to fall flat!"

With giggles and grins, they twirl and they spin,
Each little quip makes the night draw you in.
A chorus of chuckles that carry on high,
In this festive dusk where the playful birds fly.

Woodland Whimsy Unveiled

In the forest, where giggles run free,
Squirrels throw acorns with gleeful decree.
"Catch it if you can!" they jeer as they dart,
Nature's own jests are a wild work of art.

Foxes tell tales 'neath a flickering light,
"Did you see that owl? Oh, what a fright!"
They dance on their toes, a ballet of laughs,
Chasing each other through foliage paths.

A hedgehog, quite clever, takes a bold stance,
"Why do we worry when we all can prance?"
Around and around, they whirl and they play,
In this playful glen, where troubles decay.

With whispers of wind, and leaves' gentle cheer,
Woodland whimsy reigns, bringing joy near.
In a world of chuckles, we find our own song,
A chorus of laughter, where all of us belong.

Tales Told in Twilight

As twilight blankets the edge of the day,
Creatures gather 'round, with much more to say.
Frogs croak their secrets, while owls share a jest,
In the softening glow, they laugh with the best.

"Have you seen the fox with the coat of bright flame?
He thinks he's a lion—such a peculiar game!"
Choruses giggle, the laughter takes flight,
Each tale spins a sparkle, illuminating night.

Bunnies recount how they jumped their last race,
But stumbled and tumbled in a wild chase.
Every mishap brings another round cheer,
In the heart of the woods, all creatures draw near.

Under the stars, feelings warp and unwind,
As giggles bubble forth from the gentle night kind.
With wit and with warmth, they spin tales so bright,
Unraveling joys told in whimsical light.

Chuckles of the Open Glade

In the clearing where the sun beams bright,
Squirrels dance, oh what a sight!
With acorns flying all around,
Laughter echoes from the ground.

A rabbit trips, and oh dear me,
The skunks hold a wild jamboree!
With flowers worn as hats so tall,
They sing off-key, yet have a ball.

Birds crack jokes as they swoop and dive,
Teaching each other how to thrive.
While frogs croak puns, smooth as silk,
Their green tuxedos clothed in milk.

As twilight whispers secrets sweet,
The fireflies join, a glowing fleet.
In this glade, where humor thrives,
Laughter grows, and joy arrives!

Jests Among the Pine Needles

Beneath the pines, the banter flows,
The rabbit wears a hat that glows.
A raccoon hides, but peeks out sly,
With mischief sparkling in his eye.

The owls hoot riddles, wise and fun,
While chipmunks race, they've just begun.
A bear rolls down, in jest he tumbles,
Oh what a sight, as laughter fumbles!

The moose tells tales of silly fights,
While badgers play with food delights.
Each paw and claw, in joy, we share,
In this forest, humor fills the air.

As shadows stretch and crickets play,
The nightingale sings of a funny fray.
In piney realms, with giggles grand,
Together we stand, in jest we band.

The Unseen Stage of Nature

On nature's stage, where antics reign,
Animals play, engaging in grain.
A beaver builds with fateful zest,
While otters slide, they never rest.

The golden sun, a spotlight bright,
Shows hedgehogs in a silly fight.
With twirls and spins, they've mastered cheer,
Unseen applause from critters near.

The wind whispers jokes, tickles the trees,
As butterflies dance, moving with ease.
In this wild scene, all are in tune,
With laughs that echo beneath the moon.

As night blankets all in gentle hum,
The stars wink down, a joyous strum.
In this theater of woods and streams,
Laughter ignites our funniest dreams.

Banter Beneath the Boughs

Beneath the boughs, where shadows play,
  Frolicsome whispers brighten the day.
  A tortoise spins tales, slow yet grand,
While rabbits scatter, and make a stand.

  The fox and deer engage in jest,
  As the sun dips low, a playful quest.
With bouncing leaves and tumbling nuts,
  They share their tales and giggle butts.

  A squirrel tries to juggle pinecones,
With every drop, other critters groan.
    Yet in their eyes, a spark of glee,
For laughter shared is wild and free.

As twilight descends, the fun won't fade,
For every critter, in laughter, has played.
Beneath the boughs, life's joy unspools,
  In this merry realm, we're all the fools!

Mirth in the Meadow

In the meadow, sheep dance bright,
Chasing shadows in the light.
A rabbit wears a comical grin,
While butterflies sip from the gin.

A squirrel drops acorns with flair,
As frogs croak tunes without a care.
The daisies giggle as they sway,
In the funniest games of the day.

Three bees bumble, lost in song,
Thinking they're right where they belong.
But in the hive, a story unfolds,
Of honey and laughter, legends told.

So let us prance in this funny space,
Laughing loudly, weaving grace.
For in the meadow, joy is real,
In every chuckle, we find the zeal.

Tragicomedy of Twigs and Tides

On the twigs, a snail takes flight,
Wobbling left, then darting right.
A fish tells tales by the shore,
Of rainbows and clams and so much more.

The tide rolls in with a silly sound,
As seagulls gossip, circling 'round.
A raccoon slips, tumbles in the muck,
Giggling softly, what a stroke of luck!

From kelp and seaweed, laughter grows,
As crabs tap dance in silly shows.
A sea star winks, just can't resist,
In this watery play, we all persist.

So join the fun, we'll share a smile,
In this wild world, let's stay awhile.
For in this scene, both odd and grand,
We find the joy, hand in hand.

Guffaws in the Grove

In the grove, where laughter blooms,
A fox juggles with his plums.
A bear with glasses reads a book,
While wise old owls give sly looks.

The bunnies tumble without a care,
Chasing leaves that dance in the air.
A turtle mocks with a slowmo race,
While all the critters giggle in place.

Tall trees sway to the snappy beats,
As nature hums with quirky feats.
The sun plays tricks with shadows near,
Casting smiles; it's all so clear.

Thus in the grove, where joy runs free,
Laughter echoes, as it should be.
With a skip and jump, let's play along,
In this cheerful realm, we all belong.

Frolics of the Forest Floor

In the forest, giggles collide,
A hedgehog rolls with playful pride.
Mushrooms hum a lively tune,
As squirrels dance beneath the moon.

A lizard leaps with a wink and a way,
While ladybugs prance, come join the play.
The breeze tickles, makes branches sway,
With every rustle, joy finds its way.

Chasing shadows, the fireflies gleam,
Weaving together a glowing dream.
The forest floor is a stage for cheer,
An encore of laughter ringing clear.

So come together, in this brave land,
Where every creature takes a stand.
For in this frolic, oh what a score,
We find the magic forevermore.

Nature's Clown

In the woods, a squirrel prances,
Chasing shadows, lost in glances.
Invisible jester, boundless and spry,
Nuts are his jewels, oh my, oh my!

A rabbit in boots, he hops with glee,
Tap-dancing on roots, wild and free.
A chorus of birdies, singing out loud,
Nature's funny circus, so proud, so proud!

Frogs croak the tune, a ribbit parade,
While flowers in laughter sway and cascade.
The trees chuckle softly, shaking their leaves,
In the heart of the woods, joy never deceives!

So if you wander, take a glance around,
In the heart of the forest, humor is found.

The Dance of the Dappled Sun

Sunbeams spill like laughter, bright and warm,
Dancing on petals, a whimsical charm.
Leaves pirouette in a buzzing ballet,
As shadows play hide and seek in their sway.

The bumblebee buzzes with comic appeal,
Wearing a tutu, a flower to steal.
Nature's own theater, a vibrant stage,
Where jokes of the flora never age.

Squirrels share whispers, tails all a-twitch,
Nuts as their props, each one a rich pitch.
The wind gives a giggle, tickles the grass,
In this joyous realm, worries just pass.

So let the sun waltz, let the world tilt,
In the dance of the dappled, joy's always built.

Laughter Beneath the Canopy

Beneath the tall trees, the whispers ignite,
With giggles and chuckles, the day feels just right.
A gopher in glasses plays peek-a-boo,
With mushrooms as pillows, he naps in the dew.

The owls are the judges, hooting with flair,
As chipmunks tell stories, spinning through air.
A race among critters, who'll cross the line?
With acorns for medals, it's all quite divine!

The loons add their laughter upon silver lakes,
Echoes of joy in the softest of shakes.
Under leaves painted gold, every sound has its tune,
In this merry gathering, there's room for a boon.

So join the parade, let your spirit be free,
Beneath the tall trees, it's funny wildlife glee.

Whispers of the Woods

In secret, the saplings plot a surprise,
A tickle on branches, oh what a guise!
Mice in tuxedos, they hold a soirée,
With cheese on the menu, they dance and they sway.

The brook babbles jokes with a splash and a wink,
While mushrooms wear hats, they're ready to think!
A parade of odd creatures, in style so sly,
Wobbling and wobbling, they catch each eye.

Echoes of laughter, bouncing off bark,
The party persists, igniting the dark.
In the heart of this madness, joy is the theme,
Where whispers of woods turn life to a dream.

So when night falls softly, with stars sprinkled high,
Know the woods are alive; just pause and comply.

Revelry in the Relics

In the ruins, laughter rings,
A squirrel juggles shiny things,
Old stones wear a silly grin,
As echoes of joy begin.

With every crack, a tale unfolds,
Of trolls with socks and knights so bold,
The past becomes a jestful show,
Where forgotten dreams still glow.

Whispers dance like autumn leaves,
Tickling tales that no one believes,
In this playful, playful wreck,
You'll find the jesters on deck.

So gather round, let stories fly,
In these ruins, we all can sigh,
For laughter lingers, sweet and bright,
In the remnants of delight.

The Laughing Log

A log that chuckles in the sun,
Beneath its bark, a joke's begun,
With beetles clapping beetle paws,
They revel in their tiny laws.

Mice clad in acorns take a bow,
And tell their tales to every cow,
With every creak, the timber sighs,
As woodland critters crack goodbyes.

Underneath a sky so blue,
The log winks at me and you,
As laughter echoes, wild and free,
A punchline sung by every tree.

So tip your hat to this old friend,
Whose humor never seems to end,
For in its shade, we'll find the cheer,
That keeps the world just spinning here.

Glee After the Rain

Droplets dance on every leaf,
Turning gloom to comic relief,
Puddles splash in riotous bliss,
As frogs croak out their sonorous kiss.

With rubber boots and wide-eyed cheer,
Children leap without any fear,
While rainbows stretch their silly arms,
To wrap the world in sparkly charms.

A snail in haste, a laughing sight,
Slips on a mushroom in pure delight,
The earth smells fresh, the mood is light,
As colors bloom, a joyful flight.

So let the raindrops play their tune,
As giggles scatter like a balloon,
In nature's embrace, we twirl and sway,
Finding joy in every drops' display.

Chortling in the Canopy

High above where branches sway,
The birds debate the silliest play,
With every chirp and flapping wing,
Their banter makes the treetops sing.

A monkey swings with perfect flair,
His antics send the leaves in air,
As critters gather, laughter flows,
Underneath where wildness grows.

The sun peeks through in fits of glee,
As shadows dance, they tease the tree,
With every rustle, jokes unfold,
Bringing warmth in tales retold.

So join the fun beneath the boughs,
Where humor lives, and joy just vows,
In this canopy, so lush and bright,
Where chortling stars will take their flight.

Joyful Journeys through Jades

In a forest where laughter grows,
Trees wear hats made of bright bows.
Squirrels dance with jesting flair,
While wandering blooms tease the air.

Sunbeams tickle tall green grass,
Crickets chirp as friends amass.
Frogs croak jokes from muddy seats,
As giggles echo, oh, what feats!

A silly breeze pulls at my shoe,
Whispers secrets, dances too.
Every path is filled with glee,
Where joy unfolds so merrily.

So come and join the wild parade,
In jades of joy, we won't evade.
We'll twirl and whirl, forget the fuss,
In this forest, it's all a plus!

The Happiness of Hidden Hollows

In hidden nooks where giggles flow,
Nature plays, putting on a show.
A rabbit hops in socks of pink,
While shy butterflies flutter and wink.

Cartwheeling ants in a line so neat,
Caterpillars waltz to an unseen beat.
The sun peeks through a leafy dome,
Turning this hollow into a home.

Bumblebees buzz with a tiptop tune,
Singing to flowers, morning and noon.
Each shadow holds a playful tease,
Soft giggles drift on the gentle breeze.

In this place where laughter reigns,
Joyful hearts escape their chains.
Let's frolic here, beneath the boughs,
Finding happiness in nature's vows!

A Festival of Foliage

Leaves burst forth like confetti bright,
In a fest of fun, pure delight.
Dancing branches sway to the tune,
While the sky chuckles with the moon.

Golden rays in playful skirmish,
Tickling grass in joyous flourish.
Flowers sport their fanciest threads,
As laughter blossoms in their beds.

A jester robin hops with ease,
Telling tales to the swaying trees.
Nature revels, none can resist,
Join the party, it's not to miss!

In this grove of whimsical sights,
Every shadow holds giggly lights.
Come celebrate and feel the vibe,
A festival of joy, we'll imbibe!

The Lightness of Leafy Laughter

Soft whispers of leaves, a jestful crowd,
As breezes gather, swirling, loud.
A game of tag with sprightly vines,
Where each turn sparks more silly signs.

Tickled pink, the petals cheer,
With giggles ringing, far and near.
Swaying wildly, the branches play,
Dancing shadows, bright and gay.

The sun dips low, a joyful tease,
Painting the world with giddy ease.
Bouncy mushrooms join the lore,
As laughter spills from every core.

In this haven, light as air,
Joy is found everywhere.
Let's twirl with nature, laugh and run,
In leafy laughter, we are one!

The Clearing's Jest

In a glade where the squirrels jump high,
A rabbit slips under the deep blue sky.
With acorns flying, they play tag at noon,
While the old oak chuckles, a wise old tune.

A fox dons a hat, a gala in the woods,
Dancing around with the misunderstood.
The bees wear bow ties, a sweet parade,
As frogs croak laughter in the cool shade.

A snail with a top hat moves far too slow,
While mice juggle seeds in a sprightly show.
The wind adds a twist, a tickle here and there,
In this playful clearing, free from all care.

Oh, the fun never ends in this wild domain,
Where every creature joins in the entertaining chain.
With giggles and grins, the daylight retreats,
As shadows still dance to their own silly beats.

Shadows Dance with Glee

At dusk, the shadows begin their parade,
Twisting and turning through the glen they wade.
A rabbit hops high, then a tumble, oh dear,
Leaves rustle and giggle, the end of day near.

The owls hoot softly, their jokes take flight,
As the stars start to twinkle in the soft night light.
A raccoon makes mischief, a pouch full of snacks,
While whispers of laughter fill up all the cracks.

A dance-off ensues, the crickets provide,
With moonbeams illuminating the fun-filled ride.
As leaves hold their breath, so many they see,
The magic of twilight is funny and free.

In this world of shadows, where mischief abounds,
Each twirl and each giggle creates joyous sounds.
The night wears a smile, wrapped in a glee,
A perfect encore for the moonlit spree.

Frolics in the Ferns

Amongst the ferns where the sunlight is warm,
A band of small creatures begins their charm.
A hedgehog with glasses reads stories out loud,
While the critters all gather, a lively crowd.

A mouse in a bowler attempts a tightrope,
His wobbly steps fuel their laughter and hope.
Fluffy tails flutter, as they cheer and they shout,
"Just don't look down! Don't let fear creep about!"

A dance-off ignites near the ticklish roots,
With frogs in their boots and lilting flutes.
The ladybugs spin, and the beetles do twist,
In the frolicsome ferns, it's hard to resist.

The sun starts to dip, casting shadows so bold,
But the laughter of friends is a treasure of gold.
In this garden of jokes where the fables are spun,
The day fades to giggles, and the laughter has won.

Humorous Haze of the Twilight

As dusk settles in, a haze fills the air,
The critters emerge from their cozy lair.
Beneath the soft glow of the crescent moon,
They gather for stories and sing a fun tune.

With fireflies twinkling like stars come to play,
The laughter of friends lights up the gray.
A badger with bravado takes center stage,
With antics so silly, he channels his rage.

The fox twirls and dips in an unexpected jig,
While turtles join in, spinning slow like a twig.
Every twinkle and chuckle in this enchanted spot,
Is sprinkled with joy, never to be forgot.

With bursts of delight and a dash of surprise,
The evening drifts on, and no one denies.
In this hazy twilight, the friendships we find,
Are woven with laughter, pure treasures combined.

Harmony in the High Brush

In the tumble of tall grass,
Laughter echoes, loose and free,
Bumblebees dance in wild sashay,
As squirrels plot their playful spree.

A worm wears a skeptical frown,
While daisies giggle in the sun,
The wind breaks out in hearty laugh,
Nature's jokes are never done.

The brook murmurs a cheeky tune,
To frogs who croak a merry beat,
Nearby, a toad takes center stage,
With leaps that don't accept defeat.

And as the day begins to fade,
A sunset blushes in delight,
The critters share a final jest,
While the stars prepare for night.

Nature's Nuanced Nonsense

In the forest where shadows prance,
A rabbit trips over his feet,
The trees chuckle with leafy glee,
As leaves fall down in foolish defeat.

A mischievous fox draws a map,
Leading to a nonexistent prize,
He ends up lost in his own game,
With a sheepish grin and wide eyes.

A snail claims to be the fastest,
But it's just a slow-motion show,
With each slide, the crowd erupts,
In fits of laughter, row by row.

At twilight, the critters convene,
To share tales of whimsical woe,
In nature's wacky rendezvous,
Where nonsense reigns with a glow.

The Merriment of the Meadow

In meadows bright with wild delight,
Bunnies bounce with quirky flair,
Twirling round in joyful plays,
There's laughter in the fragrant air.

A butterfly slips on a flower,
Stumbling through a sweetened breeze,
While daisies hold their sides and roll,
As petals dance with perfect ease.

Grasshoppers strike a chirpy tune,
As crickets join the vivas too,
A melody of silly sounds,
In the light where laughter grew.

The sun dips low, yet spirits rise,
In whimsical twilight's soft embrace,
Where nature's humor spins a yarn,
And every heart finds its rightful place.

Twinkles and Tumbles of Terrain

On hills that wobble like jelly,
A goat takes a most daring leap,
With a twist and a turn he goes,
Into a tumble, oh so deep.

The rocks chuckle at his plight,
As he shakes off the dust and grins,
With friends below in fits of joy,
Imitating his jolly spins.

A brook races down the slope,
Splashing folks who pass in haste,
While tadpoles giggle at the chaos,
Creating waves in glee, not waste.

As stars emerge to watch the show,
Nature winks with a sparkly gleam,
For every fall, there's fun to chase,
In a landscape built from dream.

The Grinning Grove

In the grove where shadows tease,
Trees wear hats made of leaves.
Squirrels dance with acorn hats,
While rabbits laugh, they chat like chaps.

The sunbeams play a hide-and-seek,
Who knows just what they'll sneak?
A tickle from the buzzing bees,
Brings giggles floating on the breeze.

Mushrooms giggle, all in a row,
Wobbling gently, putting on a show.
A turtle slips with a comic glee,
Who would ever take him seriously?

In this grove where laughter's found,
Funny whispers dance around.
If you listen close, you might hear,
Nature's daydreams filled with cheer.

Fancies of the Fern Fronds

Ferns sway gently, they're in on the joke,
Winking at the clouds when a breeze is woke.
Sunlight flickers, shadows prance,
In the woodland, all is chance.

Bumblebees wear tiny crowns,
As they zoom above the towns.
Ladybugs play hopscotch at noon,
While crickets chirp a merry tune.

Whimsical whispers among the ferns,
Point out squirrel's curious turns.
A raccoon struts with a swaggering pace,
In a world that's full of grace.

And as the joyful echoes spread,
Unexpected guests are carefully led.
In the dance of nature's frolics bright,
Laughter glows in the golden light.

Euphoria in the Understory

In the understory, where secrets nest,
Mice play chess, they're simply the best.
Even owls giggle with a wise old wink,
While frogs croak jokes, making you think.

The mushrooms chuckle, cap to cap,
While a sleepy fox takes a nap.
All around, the laughter swells,
Each tiny critter has wondrous tales to tell.

Glimmers of joy in every nook,
Catch a glimpse like a storybook.
With laughter bubbling, a vibrant refrain,
Nature sings, delightful and insane.

In this hidden world where spirits soar,
Giggles echo, forever more.
Step lightly, friend, join the fun,
In this realm where joy's never done.

A Mischief of Melodies

In the glade where laughter sings,
A mischief of melodies takes to wings.
The wind hums a mischievous tune,
As giggling leaves sway in the afternoon.

Muskrats tap dance on a floating log,
While ducks quack rhythms, fairly in fog.
Nature's chorus, each sound a delight,
Mingle with echoes in the fading light.

Each berry bush bursts with glee,
Sending smiles for all to see.
Dandelions sway as flutes play bright,
The merriment grows, a wondrous sight.

So join the revelry, swell the cheer,
In this magical place, draw near.
With every note that takes to flight,
The forest sings, glorious and light.

The Satire of Sunbeams

Sunbeams dance upon the grass,
As squirrels scurry, quick and brash.
They trade jests beneath the trees,
While robins chirp with cheeky tease.

A rabbit hops with floppy ears,
Laughing loud, he spreads the cheers.
In this playful, sunny glade,
Humor paints the leafy shade.

Bright Boughs and Brash Smiles

Bright boughs sway with tales to tell,
Of giggles trapped in nature's swell.
A chipmunk winks, a glance so sly,
As butterflies flit quickly by.

The flowers chuckle, colors bold,
In gardens where the joy unfolds.
Every petal wears a grin,
In this playground, let's dive in.

Ease Amongst Exuberance

In a meadow where laughter grows,
The daisies dance in joyful rows.
With every breeze, a chuckle flows,
Serenity in comic prose.

Gentle whispers in the air,
Nature giggles without a care.
A brook babbles in playful rhyme,
Time slows down, sweetened by chime.

The Puns of Pine and Maple

Pine trees poke their heads up high,
Witty remarks float on by.
Maples blend their hues in jest,
A story shared, they're truly blessed.

In this forest of clever quips,
The leaves conspire in playful flips.
A beaver builds with grand designs,
Crafting puns from timber lines.

Chiming Canopies of Cheer

In the forest where giggles bloom,
Trees chuckle softly, chasing gloom.
Branches sway in a playful dance,
While squirrels plot their next mischance.

Laughter echoes through leaves up high,
A pot of joy under the sky.
Beneath the boughs, the critters meet,
Jokes exchanged, a lively treat.

Pinecones drop like comedic bombs,
Tickling toes with woodland charms.
Every rustle's a giggling sigh,
As nature's humor flutters by.

Where merriment bursts like sunlight's glow,
And silly whispers flit to and fro.
In this clearing, joy finds its head,
A riot of fun, where laughter's spread.

Revels in the Roots

Wiggling worms wear silly hats,
Hosting parties with chatty rats.
Beneath the earth is a raucous scene,
Where roots and rhymes dance in between.

Lively laughter from a burrowed den,
A riddle shared by a lively hen.
The clinking of acorns makes a sound,
Joining the fun where smiles abound.

Down in the dirt, the giggles flow,
Every pebble a punchline, don't you know?
As shadows stretch in the sunset's gleam,
The ground erupts in a joyful dream.

Emerging from greenery, a banter bright,
Sprouts of folly take flight at night.
Where laughter's the root that binds every soul,
In woodland revels, heartbeats are whole.

The Spirit of Solemnity and Smiles

In solemn shades where shadows blend,
A ticklish breeze causes all to bend.
Squirrels wearing spectacles read the trees,
Pointing out's nature's silly degrees.

A frown on a feathered face gets tossed,
As chirps of joy are happily lost.
Around the brook, the water's glee,
Reflects the chuckles from bumblebee.

Ducks waddle like they've had too much fun,
Splashing laughter under the sun.
Every ripple, a hiccup so bright,
Where solemnity fades in delight.

With giggles caught in the swirling air,
Even silence bursts with a hearty flair.
Where smiles sprout from the deep, deep ground,
And grave moments are joyously drowned.

The Jolly Veil of Vines

Vines entwine in a jolly spree,
Hugging trees with such hearty glee.
Each twist and turn has a tale to tell,
Of frolics that weave a whimsical spell.

In the canopy's charm, shadows play,
As giggles drip from light's ballet.
Caterpillars spin in a soft cocoon,
Dreaming of jokes that'll make one swoon.

The jester owl hoots in the night,
Tickling all with wisdom, quite bright.
Wit wrapped in leaves, slyly they peek,
Crafting laughter, cheeky and sleek.

Through the burlap of bark, the humor flows,
In the arms of vines, the happiness grows.
Under this jolly, joyous design,
Every spirit finds a place to shine.

The Cheerful Canopy

Beneath the leaves, a jest is spun,
Squirrels dance and birds have fun.
Laughter echoes through the trees,
Nature's giggles on the breeze.

Sunshine giggles, tickling toes,
Poppy petals strike a pose.
Clouds in costumes float so high,
Wink and wag, they drift on by.

A rabbit's prank, a sliding slope,
Caterpillars plot with hope.
The grass whispers silly plots,
As cheeky crickets play their spots.

Under the arch of cheerful light,
Life reveals its comic sight.
In this playful, leafy dome,
We laugh and sing—this is our home.

Giggles in the Greenery

In the thicket, sounds of cheer,
Bumblebees buzz, spreading cheer.
Laughter rings through ferns so bright,
Inviting all to join the light.

Frogs wear crowns of lily leaves,
Telling tales that none believe.
Every rustle, every jump,
Makes the garden wildly thump.

With tattered hats and flower blooms,
The hedgehogs plan their whirly zooms.
As daisies twirl in mock ballet,
The sun smirks, "Come out and play!"

So we gather, all aglow,
In the greenery, laughter flows.
In this wonder, let's rejoice,
Nature's humor is our choice.

Echoes of Joy in the Clear Spaces

Among the meadows, joy resounds,
Bouncing off the playful grounds.
Fiddling frogs and singing plants,
Every creature leaps and prances.

Breezes chuckle, tickling cheeks,
As butterflies share giggly streaks.
Fields alive with vibrant pranks,
Nature's humor fills the ranks.

With each twist of twig and vine,
We hear the whispers of divine.
The airy giggles float and sway,
In clear spaces, we all play.

Swinging shadows invite us near,
Where every moment's filled with cheer.
In this echo, pure delight,
We dance until the fall of night.

Whimsy Amongst the Wildflowers

In a patch of wild delight,
Petals tumble in a flight.
Bunnies bounce with playful flair,
Tiny whispers fill the air.

Sunflowers tilt, they seem to grin,
As playful breezes swirl and spin.
Their golden smiles beam so wide,
In this meadow, joy won't hide.

Ladybugs plan their tiny shows,
With winks and nods, the gossip flows.
Dancing shadows cast by bliss,
In this whimsy, we find our wish.

The wildflowers sway and sway,
Inviting hearts to laugh and play.
Here among the hues so bright,
We share in nature's pure delight.

Laughter in the Underbrush

In the thicket, giggles swell,
Critters dance, and the shadows tell.
A squirrel wears a silly crown,
While secrets tumble through the town.

The rabbit slips, lands on a vine,
A parrot squawks, this is divine!
With every tumble, every fall,
Nature's jesters entertain us all.

Mighty trees shake with delight,
Bouncing branches, what a sight!
The brook gurgles with a chuckle,
As frogs join in, they really vocal.

So wander here in playful glee,
Where laughter sings from each tall tree.
A comedy carved from earth and air,
Underbrush giggles, everywhere!

Whispers from the Woods

When the night wraps its cloak so tight,
The trees begin to share their light.
A babbling brook hums a tune,
While crickets play under the moon.

A badger struts, all pomp and pride,
While hedgehogs giggle and slide.
With every rustle, a tale unfolds,
As nature's mischief softly holds.

Whispers travel through the breeze,
Tickling ears like playful tease.
Owls exchange their evening jokes,
As shadows dance, the night provokes.

Laughter sprinkles like dew at dawn,
A symphony in the land, reborn.
So heed the whispers, oh, take a peek,
For humor blossoms where hearts speak!

Revels of the Rustling Leaves

Leaves are swirling, a playful game,
Each gust of wind beckons their name.
They twirl and tumble, a merry parade,
Nature's giggles in vibrant shades.

A fox prances, flaunting its tail,
While twigs crackle, a lively trail.
The ground beneath holds stories bold,
Of mischief woven in threads of gold.

The sun laughs down, casting beams,
While nature winks with cheeky schemes.
In every rustle, the woods erupt,
With laughter shared, joy abruptly.

With every leaf, a grin appears,
A chorus of giggles fills our ears.
So dance through rustling, playful scenes,
In the heart of nature, mirth convenes!

Mirth Beneath the Moonlight

Under the moon's soft silver glow,
Creatures plot a merry show.
Fireflies flicker, a spark of cheer,
In the stillness, laughter's near.

A mouse in boots, oh what a sight,
Dances wildly, pure delight.
Boughs bend low with gentle mirth,
As night unfolds its joyful birth.

A raccoon juggles acorns round,
While shadows sway, a playful sound.
The nightingale croons a funny song,
As the forest joins, where we belong.

So gather close, let giggles spark,
In moonlit magic, ignite the dark.
For in this realm of whimsy free,
Laughter shines, eternally!

Tickle of the Twilight Breeze

As daylight fades to pearly gray,
The breeze arrives, a playful sway.
It dances through the rustling leaves,
Whispering jokes that nature weaves.

The shadows stretch, their antics bold,
While crickets share their tales untold.
A squirrel giggles in the trees,
Chasing dreams on a cool, soft breeze.

Moonlight bathes the world in cheer,
Lighting up the laughter near.
Each star a chuckle, bright and clear,
In the twilight, fun is here.

With every rustle, every sound,
The joyous whimsy knows no bounds.
In this clearing, mirth will sing,
Embracing all that evening brings.

Revelations of Radiance

In fields adorned with golden blooms,
A band of bugs plays cheerful tunes.
Beetles tap with little feet,
As daisies sway to the lively beat.

A butterfly dons a silly hat,
And seizes day in a playful spat.
It flutters high, dips low with glee,
Teasing flowers, oh what a spree!

The sun's last wink ignites delight,
In every corner, child's laughter bright.
As if it's all a grand charade,
Where giggles grow, and woes all fade.

In this vibrant, radiant land,
Joy spills forth like grains of sand.
Every moment, a treasure to treasure,
In laughter, life finds its true measure.

A Mirthful Saunter

Through woods alive with chirps and hops,
A jovial stroll, where the laughter pops.
Beneath the boughs, a playful jest,
As nature invites us to her fest.

A rabbit trips, then straightens up,
It spins a tale, and sips from a cup.
With every twist of grass and vine,
We share a giggle, a nod, a sign.

The brook giggles as it leaps and glides,
Mirroring smiles from the world outside.
Each pebble whispers tales of glee,
In this merriment, we roam carefree.

So let us dance in this silly spree,
With every step a memory.
For in this woodland charm so bright,
Laughter is the true delight.

Glee in the Greener Pastures

In meadows wide, where daisies play,
A herd of cows brings joy our way.
With bells that chime, they sway and prance,
In this ballet of mooing dance.

The breeze is thick with cheerful sound,
As butterflies spin 'round and 'round.
Each flutter bright, a playful tease,
Bringing joy on the gentle breeze.

A goat appears, with a grin so wide,
Leading the pack with comedic pride.
For every leap, there's laughter spread,
As it bounds forth, joy is fed.

So here beneath the endless blue,
We marvel at this fun-filled view.
In greener pastures, all is right,
With laughter soaring, pure delight.

Mirth Among the Moss

In a glade where shadows dance,
Frogs in tuxedos take a chance.
Laughter bubbles, croaks abound,
As snails in bow ties spin around.

Mossy carpets soft and green,
Squirrels jive, they steal the scene.
With acorns tossed like bubbles fair,
They pirouette through fragrant air.

Giggling petals, flowers sway,
Chasing critters at play each day.
Nature grins, it's clear to see,
Joyful antics, wild and free.

Here the sun and moon partake,
In cheeky winks, in every shake.
A symphony of jest and play,
Where mossy mirth leads the way.

Tickle Tides of Twilight

Beneath the stars, a wave of cheer,
The fireflies dance, the night draws near.
Whispers float on breezes light,
As laughter rings throughout the night.

A raccoon with a hat so wide,
Invites the owls to join the ride.
They tip their hats and tilt their heads,
In a waltz beside their slumbering beds.

The moon spills giggles on the ground,
While crickets chirp a joyful sound.
And shadows play in silly games,
Each ripple of fun, it never tames.

In this twilight, joy does bloom,
Enchanted by the night's perfume.
They twirl and twist under the stars,
In a realm that's blissfully ours.

Serene Smiles of the Swamp

In the swamp where the lilies float,
An alligator learns to dote.
With a frog as his charming guide,
They set sail on a lily ride.

Marshlands echo with jovial cries,
As turtles wear their hats with pride.
Each ripple sings a merry tune,
Under the watchful, grinning moon.

With dragonflies that make a fuss,
And buzzing friends without a rush.
They gather 'round the muddy shore,
Reciting tales of days of yore.

In this sanctuary, all is light,
Where squishy feet feel just right.
Smiles abound, in every nook,
A happy look with every hook.

Bark and Banter Beneath

Beneath the canopy of glee,
Trees chuckle softly, wild and free.
With branches swaying to the beat,
The wind joins in, tapping its feet.

Squirrels scamper with tales of jest,
In nature's arms, all find their rest.
With acorn meals and mock delight,
They feast beneath the pale moonlight.

Chirps of crickets, whispers low,
A symphony in ebb and flow.
Each bark and rustle stirs the night,
With frolicsome echoes, pure and bright.

Here the woodland shares its cheer,
With every rustle, we hold dear.
In this haven, joy abounds,
A world of laughter all around.

Nonsense Amongst Nature

Silly squirrels in a dance,
Chasing shadows, take a chance.
A rabbit wears a tiny hat,
And giggles at a snoozing cat.

Fluttering butterflies in a race,
Twisting and twirling, full of grace.
A woodpecker plays tag with a bee,
While frogs croak loudly, "Join with me!"

Raccoons wearing masks of glee,
Steal an acorn, whisper, "Free!"
While jolly owls hoot in delight,
What a sight in the soft moonlight!

Pranks abound in every tree,
Nature's laughter, wild and free.
In this world where nonsense grows,
Funny tales the forest knows.

Laughing Leaves and Lively Breezes

Leaves are laughing, swirling down,
Wearing gold instead of brown.
A gust of wind, a breezy swirl,
Twirling leaves in a merry whirl.

Grasshoppers sing a silly song,
Jumping high where they belong.
A dance-off with a wandering snail,
Hopping fast, but who will fail?

The sun wiggles through the trees,
Tickling branches, 'Oh, such teasing!'.
A playful shadow on the hill,
Brings a giggle with a thrill.

Nature's joy, a grand parade,
Every creature, laughs displayed.
In the waves of grass and leaves,
Funny moments, laughter weaves.

Witty Whispers of the Wind

The wind whispers, 'Catch me quick!',
As it plays a trick so slick.
Clouds like sheep drift overhead,
Chasing dreams in their soft bed.

A feathered friend starts a jest,
While the cheeky mice just rest.
With acorns bouncing here and there,
Life's a joke in nature's fair.

Breezy giggles through the trees,
Laughter floats upon the breeze.
Every bush hides a funny face,
Nature's jokes fill every space.

Rays of sunlight beam with cheer,
As the forest lends an ear.
In the whispers, quirky tales,
With every twist, joy prevails.

The Unfolding of Foliage Fun

In the woods, a party starts,
Trees play music, sharing hearts.
Fingers of vines are swaying light,
Joining vines in pure delight.

Buds are bursting, colors bright,
Petals twirling, what a sight!
A chattering chipmunk cracks a smile,
While a snail strolls, takes its while.

Branches tickle the bluest sky,
As playful breezes whisper by.
A dance-off with a bouncing bee,
Laughing leaves are wild and free.

Nature's joy, forever spun,
From dawn to dusk, the laughter runs.
In every petal, laugh, and sun,
The unfolding of our fun begun.

Giggles of the Grass

In the meadow where daisies dance,
Laughter rises with every chance.
Bumblebees buzz a silly tune,
While crickets play beneath the moon.

Leaves sway softly in gentle glee,
As squirrels plot their next grand spree.
Beneath the sky, so wide and bright,
Nature's jesters come to light.

Fables Emerged from Foliage

Beneath the trees, tales come alive,
Silly stories that twist and thrive.
A wise old owl gives quirky advice,
While rabbits roll in fields of rice.

With nimble feet, the fox does prance,
In every corner, there's a chance.
Leaves whisper secrets, all in jest,
Nature's humor is truly the best.

Glee Mixed with Gnarled Branches

Gnarled branches twist in playful mood,
Where laughter echoes, wild and crude.
Chipmunks chatter, creating cheer,
Beneath the limbs, there's fun to hear.

The wind plays hide and seek with trees,
Tickling leaves with gentle breeze.
Every rustle holds a joke,
Nature's giggle, never broke.

The Lyricism of Laughter

In the glade where joy takes flight,
Bubbles of laughter spring, delight.
Grasshoppers leap like jokes untold,
As nature's humor unfolds bold.

Chirping birds in giggly chorus,
Bring melodies that twirl and bore us.
The world around, a stage so grand,
Where every creature plays its hand.

Lighthearted Tales from the Thicket

Amidst the brambles, laughter rings,
A squirrel juggles acorns like kings.
The rabbit slips, a tumble spree,
Chasing shadows, wild and free.

A fox in a hat struts with flair,
Reading maps with utmost care.
A dance begins, twirls all around,
Nature's jesters, joy unbound.

The birds gossip, pecking the ground,
Whispering secrets, laughter sound.
A turtle trips, its shell takes flight,
Spin and roll, oh what a sight!

In every nook, a giggle waits,
Nature's stage, and we are mates.
With every rustle, we break into cheer,
In folly's arms, we hold dear.

Capers in the Clearing

The sun peeks in, a playful tease,
A rabbit hops, brushing the leaves.
Two deer prance, showing off their grace,
Chasing shadows, a lively race.

In the clearing, a bear finds a hat,
Waddles forth, oh look at that!
With silly steps, the forest sways,
As giggles echo through leafy bays.

A chorus of critters joins the fun,
Chirping, laughing, under the sun.
In every nook, hilarity grows,
As wind whispers secrets, nobody knows.

With twinkling eyes and cheeky grins,
The woodland plays, where laughter spins.
Every creature, a partner in jest,
A clearing of joy, we are blessed.

Frogs and Fables Underfoot

Beneath the leaves, the frogs convene,
Telling tales, both quirky and keen.
A prince once kissed a toad, they say,
But hopped away, come what may!

With each croak, a story unfurls,
As dragonflies flit, and laughter swirls.
A snail in a race, oh what a sight,
Tiny champions, claiming the night.

The ants parade, bold and spry,
While grasshoppers dance, soaring high.
Who knew the ground had such delight,
In every step, a chuckle ignites!

The moon now peeks through branches wide,
Witnessing joy that cannot hide.
In the stories spun and laughter's glow,
Life in the thicket sways to and fro.

The Humor in Hidden Places

In the thicket, secrets abound,
Where giggles dance, and joy is found.
A mouse dons glasses, trying to read,
Confused by a leaf, it laughs indeed.

Not far away, a hedgehog slips,
Rolling on down, with little quips.
A gathering of creatures, all aglow,
In hidden spots, where laughter flows.

A raccoon in mischief, thieving delight,
Stashes away snacks without a fright.
With each rustle, the woods come alive,
In every corner, humor will thrive.

So let us wander, where jesters prance,
In the secret nooks, join this dance.
With hearts as light as the leaves on trees,
In hidden places, come share a tease.

www.ingramcontent.com/pod-product-compliance
Lightning Source LLC
Chambersburg PA
CBHW051651160426
43209CB00004B/880